LICHFIELD
THROUGH TIME
Anthony Poulton-Smith

AMBERLEY PUBLISHING

First published 2013

Amberley Publishing
The Hill, Stroud
Gloucestershire, GL5 4EP

www.amberley-books.com

Copyright © Anthony Poulton-Smith, 2013

The right of Anthony Poulton-Smith to be identified
as the Author of this work has been asserted in
accordance with the Copyrights, Designs and
Patents Act 1988.

ISBN 978 1 4456 0950 8

British Library Cataloguing in Publication Data.
A catalogue record for this book is available from
the British Library.

Typeset in 9.5pt on 12pt Celeste.
Typesetting by Amberley Publishing.
Printed in the UK.

Introduction

Lichfield is officially a city, albeit a small one. With a population of just 30,000, there are only six smaller in the whole of England. It gains its city status from its most famous, largest building, the cathedral. Dedicated to St Chad, being the third on this site, it is the only Medievel English cathedral with three spires, known as the Ladies of the Vale. Approaching Lichfield travellers would recognise the place immediately by its five spires – three on the aforementioned cathedral together with those of St Mary's and St Michael's churches.

However, there was a settlement here before its churches were built. Evidence of Neolithic occupation has been found, in the form of flints and stone tools, while just south of here is the village of Wall, known to the Romans as *Letocetum*. Further evidence of the importance of this area to the Romans is found in Ryknild Street and Watling Street, two of the most important Roman roads and at least as important today as the A38 and A5 trunk roads.

As the Saxon kingdom of Mercia grew in importance, so did Lichfield. King Wulfhere and King Ceolred were buried here, while King Offa raised Lichfield from a bishopric to an archbishopric, making this the Christian centre of power in England between the Humber in the north and the Thames to the south. Yet with the fall of Mercia to the Danes in the ninth century, both Lichfield and its cathedral were decimated. The see was moved to Chester and later Coventry, but restored to Lichfield in 1148.

History records very little of note in Lichfield for the next 500 years. The basic street plan of today was laid out and the settlement grew but without a sharp increase in population. Indeed the major event in this period was the fire that damaged most of the town in 1291, although it left the cathedral area largely unscathed. Not until Henry VIII's break from Rome were national problems felt locally. Its strong religious links, coupled with a major outbreak of the plague, were to prove an economical disaster.

Not until the Civil War did Lichfield play a major role in national history. Prince Rupert's Royalist forces did battle with the Parliamentarians under Lord Brooke in 1643. The latter was killed by a bullet ricocheting off nearby stonework. This was immediately hailed as a miracle and a message from God as this was St Chad's Day, the saint to whom the cathedral is dedicated. However, both seemed powerless to prevent extensive damage to the cathedral, and the central spire was completely destroyed.

Lichfield's heyday was undoubtedly the coaching era, and not simply because it stood on the busy route between London and Chester. Undoubtedly this was the catalyst for a thriving economy, and coincided with it becoming home to some of its most famous residents, including Romantic poet Anna Seward, known as the 'Swan of Lichfield'; David Garrick, the first actor to be afforded the honour of a burial in Westminster Abbey; Erasmus Darwin, a physician and founder member of the Lunar Society of Birmingham; and the best known of all, Dr Samuel Johnson, a man of letters who is often mistakenly quoted as having produced the first English dictionary when there were at least twenty earlier examples, although his was certainly the most widely imitated and used.

Much as the coaching era had been a boon for the city, the coming of the railways proved its undoing. Never a major centre for industry, the population explosion of other Midlands towns and cities, fuelled by new industries, passed Lichfield by. Indeed not until the housing developments following the Second World War did the numbers show significant growth, actually tripling in forty post-war years.

Within these pages see how parts of the city are still recognisable more than a century later. As the century enters a period of significant new development, these old and new images tell their own story of Lichfield.

Market Square

Market Square with Doctor Johnson's statue standing outside his birthplace. Lichfield's most famous resident made significant contributions to literature, as can be seen when visiting his birthplace, which is now a museum to his life.

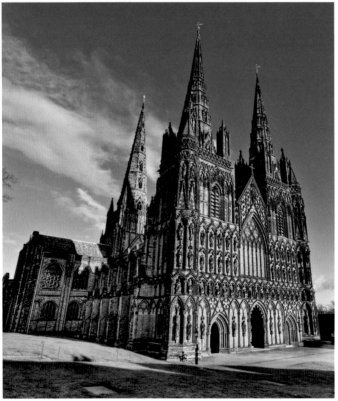

Good Stabling
The sign on the side of one of Lichfield's oldest former pubs tells us that 'Good Stabling' was available. Left, Lichfield's largest and most imposing building. Dedicated to St Chad, this is the only cathedral in the country with three spires, which are known as the Ladies of the Vale. (Courtesy of D. Lawrence)

St Mary's Church
St Mary's church was built in 1870, although there has been a church on this site since the twelfth century. It no longer holds services but houses an exhibition of the last two millennia of the city's history. It also acts as a meeting place, and has a coffee shop. (Wikimedia Commons)

Dr Johnson's Birthplace
Samuel Johnson's birthplace, now a museum to his life. Born here on 18 September 1709, in the upper floors above his father's bookshop, he was such a sickly baby his aunt is held to have commented at his birth how she 'would not have picked up such a poor creature in the street'. (Wikimedia Commons)

Conduit Street

Conduit Street got its name from a water channel which drained water away from the city for many years. This view looks back towards where the clock tower once stood. It is one of the few parts of the city centre where little of the early image remains. (Wikimedia Commons)

Dr Samuel Johnson's Statue
Samuel Johnson's statue in Market
Square by Richard Cockle Lucas
in 1838. Johnson is depicted
seated on a Greek Revival chair,
beneath which are some of the
numerous works he consulted and
read in producing his dictionary.
(Wikimedia Commons)

The Clock Tower
The Clock Tower was erected in 1863 and has a Grade II listing. When traffic increased the whole construction was removed to its present location at the Festival Gardens. (Wikimedia Commons)

Ladies of the Vale
Lichfield Cathedral from the south-east. It is famous for being the only Medieval English cathedral in the country with three spires, known as the Ladies of the Vale. (Courtesy of Lichfield District Council)

Garden of Remembrance

Lichfield Cathedral, thought to date to the late eighth century, is seen below in the modern era to the rear of Lichfield's Garden of Remembrance. (Courtesy of Lichfield District Council)

Greenhill Bower
Greenhill Bower seen outside the Empire Theatre on 1 June 1903. Below, the former cinema was once a magnet for movie-goers. Later, it was home to a branch of Kwiksave and at the time of writing is rumoured to be in line for refurbishment as a hotel. (Courtesy of Lichfield District Council)

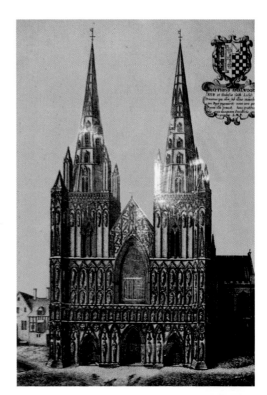

Cathedral Close

An engraving depicting the front aspect of Lichfield Cathedral, and looking back along the Cathedral Close today. (Courtesy of Lichfield District Council)

City of Lichfield
A spitfire named *City of Lichfield* flew during the Second World War. Below, the men honoured by the city's Garden of Remembrance, seen through the impressive gate. (Courtesy of Lichfield District Council)

The Close
The Close, probably from between the wars if the car is represented accurately. Below, a view of the three spires from across Beacon Park. (Courtesy of Lichfield District Council)

Stowe Street

Stowe Street, 1817. This street is almost unrecognisable today, save for Cruck House which would have been an old building even when the first image was drawn. (Courtesy of Lichfield District Council)

Sheriff's Ride

A snapshot of the Sheriff's Ride in 1908. This 20-mile annual event features fifty riders and is held on the Saturday nearest to 8 September. Queen Anne's charter of 1553 separated Lichfield from the rest of Staffordshire, effectively making it a county in its own right, by which time the Tudor House below had already stood for forty-three years. (Courtesy of Lichfield District Council)

Sadler Street and Cruck House

Sadler Street pictured in 1816, by which time Cruck House (*below*) was already at least 400 years old. During redevelopment work in the 1950s this fourteenth- or fifteenth-century timber-framed building was found encased in the 'shell' of a much more recent construction. Demolition was halted and preservation work resulted in the popular meeting place we see today. (Courtesy of Lichfield District Council)

Dam Street

Dam Street in 1813 and again today. Long an important thoroughfare in the city, it was home to Dr Samuel Johnson's first school. Aged six or seven, Johnson, whose eyesight was quite poor, would normally be met by a household servant at the end of the school day to lead him the short distance home. When the servant failed to show one day, Johnson began crawling home to avoid tripping over the many ruts and channels in the road surface. His teacher, Anne Oliver, had noticed his plight and was following him from a short distance until Johnson was suddenly aware of her witnessing his humiliation. He stood and raced back to her where he began kicking and punching the poor woman. (Courtesy of Lichfield District Council)

Sandford Street

Sandford Street in 1817 and again during the twenty-first century. Several buildings are common to both, most notably the building at the forefront on the right and, next door, the Horse and Jockey public house, which the archway reveals as a coaching inn of two centuries earlier. (Courtesy of Lichfield District Council)

Greenhill
Greenhill at the beginning of the nineteenth and twenty-first centuries. The area where the children are playing has been developed, contrasting with the obviously older houses on the left. (Courtesy of Lichfield District Council)

Beacon Street

Beacon Street in 1817 and the modern era. Interestingly, it was known as Bacon Street in the earlier image, as it had been for centuries, and the 'e' was not added until 1836. This was because cured meat was sold and/or produced here. (Courtesy of Lichfield District Council)

St John's Hospital

St John's Hospital around 1833. These almshouses are descended from the priory dedicated to St John the Baptist, founded by Bishop Roger de Clinton in 1129 and completed in 1135. At that time visitors to the city would not be permitted to enter the city gates during the hours of darkness; the priory outside the Culstubbe Gate afforded overnight hospitality as the Hospital of St John the Baptist Without the Barrs of the City of Lichfield. (Courtesy of Lichfield District Council)

Dr Johnson's Willow
This remarkably large willow had
a girth of 21 feet at head height,
and was first recorded as Johnson's
Willow in 1810. Fifteen years later
the already rotting tree was uprooted
by a severe storm; however, a single
healthy branch was cut and planted
in the same place where it thrived.
Spires can be seen in the background.
(Courtesy of Lichfield District Council)

Beacon Park
A view from the west
in 1843. An avenue
of trees make for
a delightful walk
through Beacon Park.
(Courtesy of Lichfield
District Council)

Sheriff's Ride, 1908

The Sheriff's Ride at the Guildhall in 1908. Today the Ride still departs here at 10.30 a.m. and returns eight hours later. The route takes in lunch at Freeford Manor and tea at Pipe Hall, before being met by sword and mace bearers and escorted to the Cathedral Close to meet the Dean and then back to their starting point. Below, the Corn Exchange building today. (Courtesy of Lichfield District Council)

Lichfield Cathedral
Lichfield Cathedral in the first half of the nineteenth century and again today. Built from sandstone quarried locally, the walls of the nave lean slightly outwards owing to the weight of the roof they support. During renovation work between 200 and 300 tons of stone were removed to resolve this problem. (Courtesy of Lichfield District Council)

Lichfield Cathedral, West Front
Lichfield Cathedral from the west front.
Above the door are a row of figures,
each housed in their own nook. The
central image above the door is that of
St Chad heading a line including every
early king of England. (Courtesy of
Lichfield District Council)

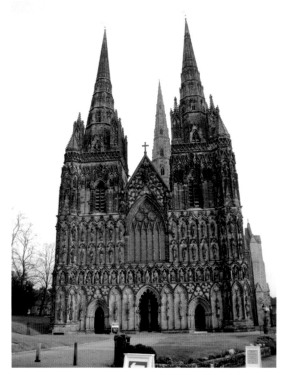

Bore Street, 1817
Bore Street, first mentioned in 1506, is pictured in 1817 and 2012. It gets its name from the boards laid along as an early pavement, raising pedestrians above the mud and filth of the street. (Courtesy of Lichfield District Council)

Conduit Street, 1817
Conduit Street, as with Bore Street, pictured in 1817 and in 2012. The Corn Exchange was built in 1849 and is one of many listed buildings in the city. It was built by T. Johnson & Son and includes lettering telling it acted as the 'Corn Exchange, Market Hall and Savings Bank'. (Courtesy of Lichfield District Council)

Milley's Hospital
Milley's Hospital, Beacon Street, and the former Probate Court building which stands on the site of the home of David Garrick. This was demolished in 1856 and replaced by Baker's Lane. (Courtesy of Lichfield District Council)

Baker's Lane
Baker's Lane can probably boast the most changed street in the city. Obviously once known for its many bakers and their produce, today it is the main thoroughfare of the city's Three Spires shopping centre. (Courtesy of Lichfield District Council)

St Mary's Church Tower

St Mary's church tower still overlooks Dr Johnson's statue, but Lichfield's most famous son would not recognise this building. The present church, the fifth on this site, was built in 1868. Today it houses the Lichfield Heritage Centre, a superb exhibition containing the history of the city from its earliest days. (Courtesy of Lichfield District Council)

Cathedral School

Lichfield Cathedral from the south-east in 1840. The view of the Cathedral School and its front shows it is home to well-established wisteria. (Courtesy of Lichfield District Council)

Gaia Lane

From Stowe to Lichfield, said to be the favourite walk of Samuel Johnson, who would also have known Gaia Lane. Certainly this has some connection with religion; Gaia was the personification of Mother Earth in Greek mythology but how this became linked to a region dominated by the cathedral and St Chad's is unclear. (Courtesy of Lichfield District Council)

Colonel Swinfen Broun
A painting of Colonel Swinfen Broun, and below, Donegal House where a clock hangs after being donated to the borough in 1928 by his descendant, Mr M. A. Swinfen Broun. (Courtesy of Lichfield District Council)

Swans and Cattle
A pool with swans and a boatman in the nineteenth century. Below, the entrance to the close today with (*inset*) a warning that the droving of cattle through the close is still not permitted. (Courtesy of Lichfield District Council)

THE CLOSE
NOTICE
The Road through the Close
not being a Public thoroughfare
no WAGGONS, CARTS & CATTLE
are allowed to pass through.
By Order of the Dean & Chapter

The Sound of Bells
Lichfield Cathedral, 1908, and looking
across the rooftops on a Sunday morning.
Sadly the photograph does not record the
joyous sound of the bells. (Courtesy of
Lichfield District Council)

The Guildhall
The Guildhall today contains a small museum showing a little of what life would have been like for the prisoners. (Courtesy of Lichfield District Council)

Bird Street

The old library and museum in Bird Street has hardly changed on the outside although today it houses the Registry Office. (Courtesy of Lichfield District Council)

St Chad's

St Chad's at Stowe contains a memorial to Lucy Porter, Dr Samuel Johnson's stepdaughter. It boasts four bells: three from the seventeenth century and the other cast in 1255. (Courtesy of Lichfield District Council)

Conduit Street Archways

From Conduit Street in 1843 to the modern view we see that the archways on both the left and the right are still making it difficult for pedestrians to pass in opposite directions. (Courtesy of Lichfield District Council)

Wade Street

Wade Street in 1818 is completely unrecognisable 200 years later. It gets its name from nearly always being extremely wet, as can be seen in the picture below. (Courtesy of Lichfield District Council)

Nave and North Transept
The nave and north transept of Lichfield Cathedral in 1840. This is one of the oldest buildings in Quonians Lane. (Courtesy of Lichfield District Council)

Western Doorway of Lichfield Cathedral The ornate, symmetrical lines of architecture as seen in the western door of the cathedral in the nineteenth century contrast with the temporary plain glass windows of Lady Chapel in the modern era, as the original stained glass windows are currently being repaired and cleaned as part of major restoration work. (Courtesy of Lichfield District Council)

Statues
Dr Samuel Johnson's statue in the
Market Place around 1820. Below,
a man who was never associated
with Lichfield, but the city was
chosen for its central location within
Staffordshire and good transport links,
Captain Smith, the man in charge
of the most famous ship in history,
RMS *Titanic*, on its maiden voyage.
(Courtesy of Lichfield District Council)

Prince of Wales
The Prince of Wales, future
Edward VII, stands on the steps
of Lichfield Cathedral. Below,
Quonians Lane again, and an old
place of worship with the image
on the wall (*inset*). (Courtesy of
Lichfield District Council)

West Gate in Cathedral Close
The West Gate in Cathedral Close in the early nineteenth century. This, the third cathedral on this site, is by far the largest. At 370 feet in length and with a central spire of the cathedral rising to 252 feet, and two further spires measuring 190 feet, this is one of the nation's oldest places of worship. (Courtesy of Lichfield District Council)

Sheriff's Ride and the Old Grammar School

The Sheriff's Ride in 1908 would have recognised the modern rear view of the council chambers. The latter is housed in the Old Grammar School and Schoolmaster's House, both built in 1682. (Courtesy of Lichfield District Council)

Relics of Yesteryear
Whit Monday celebrations and two relics of yesteryear: a part of the ancient wall of Lichfield Friary, founded in 1229 and ended with the Dissolution of the Monasteries; with a more modern relic, a red telephone kiosk. (Courtesy of Lichfield District Council)

Bird Street

Bird Street, 1816, and just past the modern Garden of Remembrance, a reminder that part of Lichfield's history still exists beneath the feet of innumerable pedestrians coming past here each year. (Courtesy of Lichfield District Council)

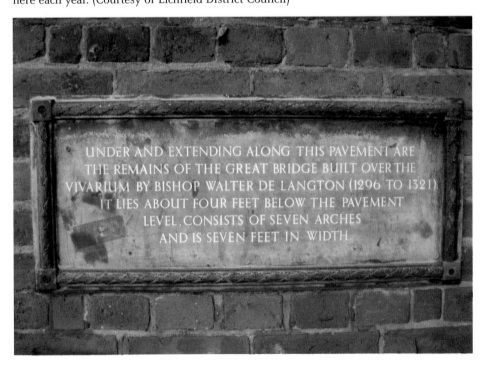

UNDER AND EXTENDING ALONG THIS PAVEMENT ARE
THE REMAINS OF THE GREAT BRIDGE BUILT OVER THE
VIVARIUM BY BISHOP WALTER DE LANGTON (1296 TO 1321)
IT LIES ABOUT FOUR FEET BELOW THE PAVEMENT
LEVEL.CONSISTS OF SEVEN ARCHES
AND IS SEVEN FEET IN WIDTH

St John Street in 1816 and Today
St John Street in 1816 and today is marked by the unchanged and easily recognised chimney stacks. At the time of the earlier image each almsman received three shillings and sixpence (17.5p) per week for maintenance, some sixteen shillings (80p) per annum for coal, and pocket money amounting to a whole shilling (5p) each and every year! (Courtesy of Lichfield District Council)

The Friary
Lichfield Cathedral and a view of the Friary. This building is now occupied by the local library and Lichfield's Record Office. In recent years the outside has received a much-needed facelift. (Courtesy of Lichfield District Council)

The Market House
The Market House in the early part of the nineteenth century, when Causeway House in Dam Street would certainly have been home to those who shopped in the Market Place. (Courtesy of Lichfield District Council)

Deadeye Dick
Permanent Library in 1833 and the doorway where, on 2 March 1643, Lord Brooke was shot and killed by a sniper who had positioned himself on the battlements of the cathedral with the sole intention of annoying the enemy. An excellent shot indeed by Mr Richard Dyott and some maintain this is the origin of the phrase 'Deadeye Dick'. (Courtesy of Lichfield District Council)

Schools

Minors School in 1833 and the former grammar school and Headmaster's House (now home to the Lichfield Council offices) in 2013. (Courtesy of Lichfield District Council)

The Old Grammar School
The Old Grammar School, along with the present-day Samuel Johnson Community Hospital, where new buildings in the foreground have been carefully designed to fit in with the originals in the background. (Courtesy of Lichfield District Council)

Lichfield Grammar School in 2013

Lichfield Grammar School is much harder to capture in 2013 owing to the increase in traffic. Included among its more famous former pupils are Elias Ashmole, David Garrick, Samuel Johnson and Joseph Addison. (Courtesy of Lichfield District Council)

Restoration
Restoration of the cathedral spire and
a modern view across the rooftops to
the spire of St Mary's. (Courtesy of
Lichfield District Council)

The First Lift
Dr Samuel Johnson's birthplace from a painting by Edward Hull dated around 1870. Below, the first building in Lichfield to boast a lift; it is now a gents outfitters. (Courtesy of the Samuel Johnson Birthplace Museum)

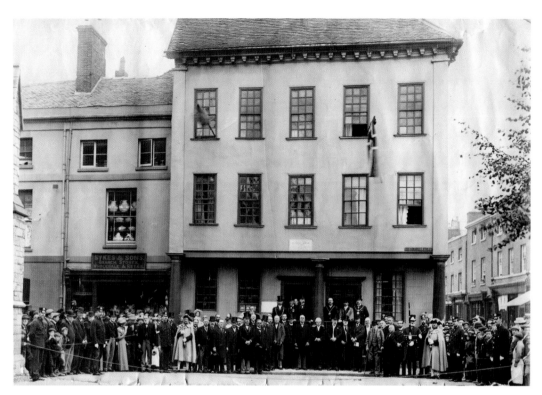

John Gilbert

A civic party and spectators assembled outside Dr Johnson's birthplace. This was taken on 18 September 1900, when John Gilbert handed over the deeds to the property, which he had purchased for the city, and received the Freedom of Lichfield in thanks. Right, the former site of Dame Oliver's Infant School in Dam Street where Samuel Johnson was taught English in 1714. (Courtesy of the Samuel Johnson Birthplace Museum)

Wissage Road
Lichfield's grammar school around 1830. Perhaps one of these boys lived in Wissage Road, where old and new houses blend well, although the meaning of its name is completely unknown. (Courtesy of the Samuel Johnson Birthplace Museum)

Lichfield Trent Valley Railway Station
An image of Lichfield Trent Valley railway station from the days of steam, and seen in the modern era where only the tracks are recognisable today. (Courtesy of the Samuel Johnson Birthplace Museum)

Market Place and Friary Remains
Lichfield's Market Place during the lifetime of Dr Johnson from a painting by Mr Paul Braddon, long after the friary had disappeared, although some remains can still be found. (Courtesy of the Samuel Johnson Birthplace Museum)

Market Place and Market Street

The Market Place in 1831 and Market Street today have not always been a place to do the shopping. During the reign of Mary I (aka Bloody Mary) Thomas Hayward, John Goreway and Joyce Lewis were burned at the stake here. Then in 1612, having been found guilty of heresy, Edward Wightman suffered a similar fate; he was the last man in England to be burned at the stake for heresy. (Courtesy of the Samuel Johnson Birthplace Museum)

Stowe Pool
Johnson's Willow, St Chad's church and Stowe House, from a painting by an unknown artist. The view across Stowe Pool today is one where water is dominant. (Inset picture courtesy of the Samuel Johnson Birthplace Museum)

West Front of Lichfield Cathedral
The west front of the Cathedral of St
Chad's as seen from the close. The
buildings have changed little in almost
two centuries. (Courtesy of the Samuel
Johnson Birthplace Museum)

Days of Steam
Another reminder of the days of steam at Lichfield Trent Valley. Today the station's name is displayed in stone.

Johnson's Willow

Johnson's Willow looking across to St Chad's church beyond. Few outside the city realise this is the official parish church. Founded in 669 as St Mary's, it was re-dedicated in the name of its founder who baptised converts to Christianity in the nearby waters. (Courtesy of the Samuel Johnson Birthplace Museum)

Samuel Johnson
Samuel Johnson as depicted in a painting by Joshua Reynolds. The good doctor would have been aware of the importance of the Crucifix Conduit bringing fresh water into Lichfield; the modern drinking fountain represents this source of fresh water, which was available from 1301 to 1928. (Courtesy of the Samuel Johnson Birthplace Museum)

Lichfield Canal

Lichfield's canals were once important for transport. Today canals are used strictly for leisure purposes and work continues on reopening the Lichfield Canal at Borrocop Locks, which have been partially filled with water. (Courtesy of the Samuel Johnson Birthplace Museum)

David Garrick
David Garrick as depicted in 1776
in a painting by William Pether.
The premier theatre venue today is
aptly named the Lichfield Garrick.
(Courtesy of the Samuel Johnson
Birthplace Museum)

Erasmus Darwin
Joseph Wright painted this image of
Erasmus Darwin towards the end of
his life in 1802. Below is the home
that bears his name, Darwin House.
(Courtesy of the Samuel Johnson
Birthplace Museum)

Richard Cockle Lucas
Richard Cockle Lucas returns to
Lichfield to maintain the statue he had
created. As he brought along a camera
to record the event he also managed to
create one of the earliest photographs
ever taken in Lichfield and, arguably,
the oldest surviving image of the
city. The modern photograph is that
of Boswell, Johnson's biographer.
(Wikimedia Commons)

Bishop's Palace

The Bishop's Palace replaced the earlier residence built by Bishop Langton in the fourteenth century. It was the official residence of the bishop from the 1860s until 1954, and is now Lichfield Cathedral School.

The Clock Tower Moved

Lichfield's clock tower was erected in 1863 in Bore Street, only to be relocated in 1928 to the Friary as traffic problems grew. Originally it had been planned to incorporate the state of Samuel Johnson in the Market Place in the proposed town clock, which may well have meant the tower would never have had to be moved.

Rail Distances

Lichfield Trent Valley railway station was opened on 15 September 1847 as part of the line to connect the London & Birmingham Railway at Rugby to the Grand Junction Railway at Stafford, and was situated approximately half a mile north of the present station, which first saw the light of day in 1871. The modern station gives the rail distance to two important destinations.

Pools

Stowe Pool was once simply a millpond but, from 1856, it became a reservoir for fresh water, although it has not been used as a source since 1968. Below is Minster Pool, again originally a millpond, used from the eleventh century to feed a mill that was demolished in 1856. Both pools are now only used for public amenities.

Trent Valley/City

Lichfield City railway station was opened in 1849, originally to serve the South Staffordshire Railway from Lichfield Trent Valley station to Walsall and Dudley. Since 1968 the station has been the terminus for the line from Birmingham, although trains do also connect to Lichfield Trent Valley.

St Michael's Church

St Michael's church was first built in the twelfth century, although much of what we see today dates from the restoration of the 1840s. However, it is the churchyard which attracts the most interest, as today it is one of the largest in the country at 9 acres, and can also boast of being one of the five oldest burial grounds in England.

Tamworth Street

Tamworth Street (*above*) is shown with a cross on John Speed's map of 1610 near the junction with Lombard Street. This may indicate that it was a route followed by pilgrims visiting the tomb of St Chad.

ECCLESIÆ CATHEDRALIS LICHFELDENSIS
a Meridie Profpectus

The Pig and Truffle

Again Tamworth Street below. Despite its appearance, the Pig and Truffle would not have offered refreshment to those travelling the route on a pilgramage to the tomb of St Chad and his cathedral, as this is a modern idea of a traditional pub name and frontage. Pigs were once used to hunt out this delicacy until it was realised dogs were equally as skilled – and wouldn't eat the truffle!

Bird Street

Modern Bird Street (*above*) appears as Friers
Alley on Speed's map of 1610 and later as
Moss Alley. It is first referred to as Byrd
Street in a document dating from 1506 and
likely named after a family named Bird,
as indeed was Moss Alley. The alternative
name of Friers Alley shows this was
associated with the cathedral, which, were
it not for the modern buildings, would be
visible on the right of the modern image.

Impressive Buildings

Master's House was given a Georgian facelift by Edmund Outram in the 1820s at a cost of £1,200. It had previously been home to the Weston family and, although the original date is uncertain as there has been so much building work done here, is thought to date from at least the sixteenth century.

Marlborough House
Marlborough House was built in 1740, although additions in the late eighteenth and early twentieth century were designed to meld seamlessly with the original architecture.

LICHFIELD CATHEDRAL "CENTRAL SPIRE DISMANTLED" 1949

Cathedral Repairs
Repairs underway at the cathedral just after the Second World War, which would have pleased St Chad himself.

Number 53 Bore Street

Number 53 Bore Street was home to Compton's Accessories in 1932. The present Mr Simms Olde Sweet Shoppe is a modern chain of shops where sweets are sold in the traditional style. (Courtesy of D. Lawrence)

The Old Crown Hotel
The Crown Hotel around the time of the Second World War; this building was demolished in 1983. Left, another royal landmark: the statue of Edward VII in Beacon Park. (Courtesy of D. Lawrence)

Tamworth Street

Tamworth Street between the wars, with repair work proceeding as usual. Seen right is the old borough seal. It shows 'the field of the dead', once thought to be the origin of the place name of Lichfield – it actually means 'the grey field' – and based on the legend that a thousand Christians were martyred around AD 300. (Courtesy of D. Lawrence)

Birmingham Road

Birmingham Road and the Apex Garage back when petrol pumps were aesthetically pleasing. Below, the Horse & Jockey public house reminds us Lichfield Races were a large annual attraction. (Courtesy of D. Lawrence)

General View Museum Grounds Lichfield

Beacon Park

Above, the museum gardens, Beacon Park, thought to be around the beginning of the twentieth century. Below, a view of Jubilee Gardens today. (Courtesy of D. Lawrence)

British Legion
The former British Legion building in Beacon Street. Below, inside the St John's almshouses, a place of peace and quiet. Both have been most benevolent towards Lichfieldians for many years. (Courtesy of D. Lawrence)

Henry Hall
Henry Hall, father of Louise, who still owns Dame Oliver's, working at his butcher's shop in Market Square and Pool House in Dam Street. (Courtesy of Louise of Dame Oliver's in Dam Street)

St Chad's Well
St Chad's Well, a place of pilgrimage since the nineteenth century. The earlier stone construction was demolished in 1949 and replaced by the modern version. (Wikimedia Commons)